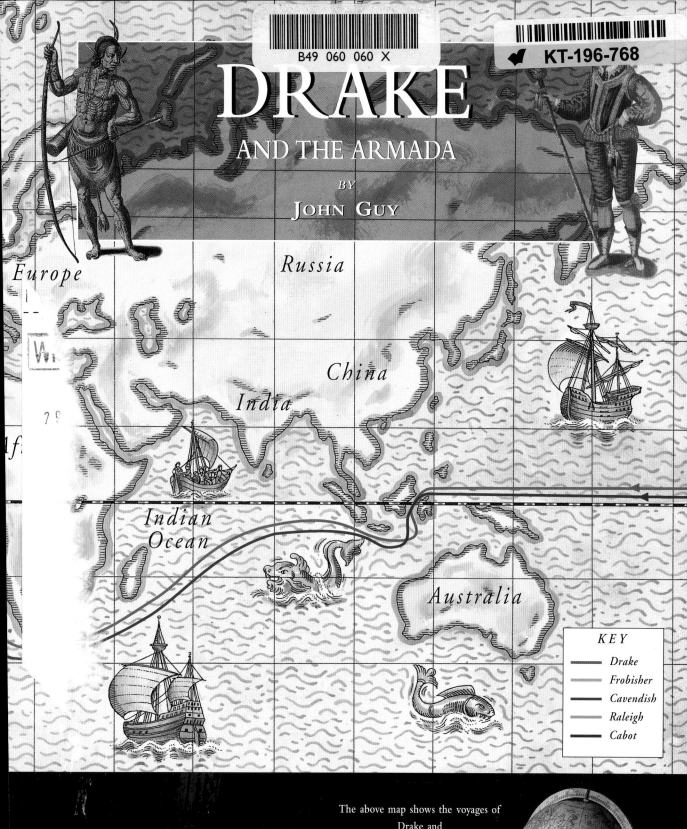

DRAKE
AND THE ARMADA

BY

JOHN GUY

Europe

Russia

China

India

Indian
Ocean

Australia

KEY

	Drake
	Frobisher
	Cavendish
	Raleigh
	Cabot

The above map shows the voyages of
Drake and
other Elizabethan explorers.

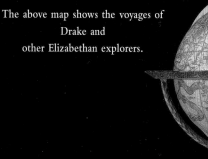

THE EARLY YEARS

DEFENDING THE FLEET

When Drake's father arrived in Kent he became preacher in Chatham Dockyard. In 1560 he became vicar of Upchurch, and young Francis first learned his sailing skills on the River Medway.

*S*ir Francis Drake is best remembered for his defeat of the Spanish Armada, his circumnavigation of the world, and his daring raids on the Spanish in the Caribbean. He was born into a humble family in Devon and grew up in Kent. They lived for some years on board a hulk (an old ship) moored on the River Medway, where Francis learned to sail. Later, he was apprenticed to the captain of a trade ship. Then his distant cousin, John Hawkins, found him a position on a slave-trading voyage and Drake soon rose to the rank of captain.

CHILDHOOD HOME

Francis Drake was born at Crowndale, near Tavistock in Devon, some time between 1539 and 1545, the eldest of 12 children. This statue was later erected in Tavistock in honour of Drake's achievements.

DRAKE'S ISLAND

In 1549 the Drake family was forced to seek refuge on St Nicholas' Island, Plymouth Harbour. The island was afterwards known as 'Drake's Island' to commemorate the event.

EVENTS OF DRAKE'S LIFE

~1492~
Columbus's first voyage to the West Indies

~1519~
Magellan sets out on first circumnavigation of the world

~1533~
Princess Elizabeth (later Elizabeth I) is born

A TRADE OF MISERY

John Hawkins began his successful career like many others, working in the slave trade in 1562. Drake's first such voyage was aboard one of Hawkins's ships in 1566. The voyage itself ended in disaster, but Drake went on to become an officer, and in 1568 took command of his first ship.

IRISH REVOLTS

In 1573, on his return from raiding Spanish ships in the Caribbean, Drake was sent to Ireland. Queen Elizabeth had made a peace with Spain and Drake would have been an embarrassment at court. He stayed there for three years, helping put down Irish rebellions.

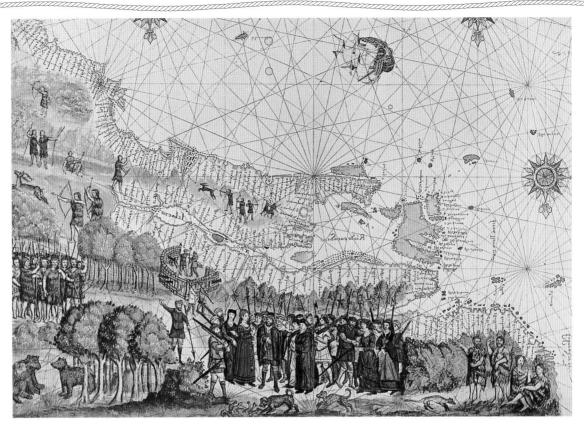

JACQUES CARTIER (1491-1557)

Jacques Cartier was a French explorer searching for new sites to settle in North America. He made several journeys around north-east America and in 1534 circumnavigated the Gulf of St Lawrence. He is seen here on a later expedition in 1542, landing on the banks of the mighty St Lawrence River. Cartier's explorations led to the French claims on Canada.

EVENTS OF DRAKE'S LIFE

-1541-

Probable year of Drake's birth

-1545-

Henry VIII's ship the *Mary Rose* sinks

-1547-

Henry VIII dies

-1549-

Drake family (Protestants) forced to leave Devon for Kent

-1553-

Edward VI dies and is succeeded by Mary I

CHALLENGING SEAS

The northern Atlantic and Arctic Oceans are difficult to sail. Icebergs were a problem and vast areas iced over completely in winter. This made it difficult for early explorers to chart the northern coasts of America and Russia. The search for both the North-East and North-West Passages led to the same place – later named the Bering Strait.

NEW TRADE ROUTES

— *Frobisher (1576)* — *Hudson (1610-11)* — *Cartier (1534-6)*

Together, Spain and Portugal controlled the southern seaways, forcing other nations to search for an alternative route to reach the Pacific Ocean and the riches of China and south-east Asia. Two possibilities emerged: the North-East Passage, (around the northern coasts of Russia), and the North-West Passage, (around the northern coasts of North America). Having attacked Spanish ports off South America, Drake headed home, but was forced back across the Pacific and so (unintentionally) sailed home round the world. The Norwegian explorer, Roald Amundsen, was the first person to sail round northern Canada and through the Bering Strait in 1906.

THE FUR TRADE

As they could not get to China and the Far East, merchants turned to North America and the fur trade (and later gold). Large companies such as the Hudson Bay Company, made huge profits buying animal pelts cheaply from the native Americans and then exporting them to Europe.

HENRY HUDSON

Henry Hudson was an English explorer employed by the Dutch East India Company to search for the North-West Passage. After several attempts he discovered what are now known as the Hudson River, Strait and Bay. In 1611 his crew mutinied and cast him adrift in a small boat with eight others. He was never seen again.

NEAR MISS

One of the problems facing 16th-century explorers was that the lands they were searching for were completely unknown in terms of location and size. On his journey home round the world, for example, Drake sailed a zigzag course through the East Indies taking him very close to Australia's northern coast.

THE GOLDEN HIND

Drake's ship was originally called the *Pelican*, but he renamed it *Golden Hind* before setting off across the southern oceans. This was in honour of his patron, Sir Christopher Hatton, whose coat of arms included a hind.

CENTRE OF THE UNIVERSE

In Elizabethan times, the other planets in our solar system were thought to revolve around the Earth. Armillary spheres were used to show the heavenly bodies and relative positions of the Equator, the Tropics, Arctic and Antarctic circles. After Magellan successfully circumnavigated the world, it became possible to draw more precise navigational charts.

THE FIRST ENGLISHMAN IN JAPAN

Will Adams set sail in 1598 to south-east Asia. Only one of the five ships that set out survived, eventually landing in Japan in 1600. Adams was taken prisoner, but later released on condition he taught the Japanese his seafaring skills.

SOUTHERN CONTINENT

Drake (1577-80)

While few Europeans suspected that North and South America existed in the 16th century, there were tales of a huge 'Southern Continent' somewhere in the South Atlantic. Many thought it was the lost continent of Atlantis and several attempts were made to find it. At the same time, the explorers were also hoping to make trading links with south-east Asia, especially the Spice Islands, China and Japan. By the end of the 16th century Spain's 'golden age' was coming to a close. Most of the discoveries made after then were by English, Dutch and French expeditions.

'LOST' CONTINENT

Although a few explorers had found the islands north of Australia, they could not find an inhabited southern continent. Dutchman, Abel Tasman landed in Australia in 1642 (right). Much later, in his own voyages of 1768-80, Captain Cook finally proved that there was no southern continent and the full outline of Australia was charted.

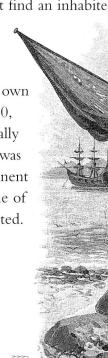

AROUND THE WORLD

Francis Drake was the first Englishman to successfully circumnavigate the world. The main reason for Drake's great journey, however, was for trade and plunder. At the time, Spain was the most powerful nation in Europe and guarded the seaways to her new colonie Elizabeth I asked Drake to sail across the southern Atlantic, through the Straits of Magellan, and attack Spanish treasure ships and settlements on South America's west coast. He then went on to cross the Pacific Ocean and reach the Spice Islands of the East Indies. Drake returned home a very rich man.

'THE DRAGON'

Drake had a strong personality and people respected him. Native peoples often worshipped him and the Spanish called him *El Draque* – 'the Dragon'.

LOST CIVILIZATION

The Mayan civilization of Central America flourished many centuries before Drake's circumnavigation. They understood astronomy and mathematics, but like the Spanish. he just plundered their riches. The round tower shown here is an observatory at the Mexican city of Chichen Itza.

SPANISH GOLD

Spain plundered the wealth of the nations of Central and South America. Gold ornaments were melted down and natives set to work in gold and silver mines. The riches shipped back to Spain interested Drake and the other Elizabethan privateers. The coins shown here are doubloons (meaning a double or two-escudo piece), the highest value Spanish coin at that time.

NEW ALBION

Drake stopped at what is now San Francisco to refit his ships before starting the journey home. He met the local Indians, who invited him to become their king. He refused, but claimed the area for England (calling it New Albion). The Spanish made several explorations up the Californian coast, built a small missionary settlement there by the bay, and called it San Francisco.

REVENGE

Here, Brazilian cannibals allow missionaries to baptise their prisoners but only with a damp cloth so as not to spoil the flavour.

AZTEC SPLENDOUR

This picture of Tenochtitlan, in Mexico, shows the magnificent Aztec capital city.

EVENTS OF DRAKE'S LIFE

~1565~
Tobacco introduced into England

~1566~
Drake's first voyage to the Caribbean as junior officer

~1569~
Drake marries Mary Newman at St Budeaux, near Plymouth

~1570~
Drake sails for the coast of Panama and begins his reign of terror amongst Spanish shipping

~1572~
Drake sets out to take the Spanish port of Nombre de Dios, in Panama

~1573~
Peace is agreed between England and Spain

~1576~
Martin Frobisher attempts to find North-West Passage

SEARCH FOR THE WAY HOME

There is some argument about the exact route home taken by Drake. Some claim that he did not touch land again after leaving Java until arriving back at Plymouth. Others believe he may have visited southern India before crossing the Indian Ocean.

THE GOLDEN HIND

Drake set sail from Plymouth on 13 December 1577 with five ships. His flagship was the *Pelican*, a small vessel of 108 tonnes and carrying just 18 cannon. The smallest ship, the *Benedict*, was just 13 tonnes – a tiny vessel for such a journey. About half way into the journey, Drake abandoned two of his ships. Of the other three, the *Marigold* sank and the *Elizabeth* returned to England. Only the flagship, renamed the *Golden Hind*, completed the circumnavigation.

KNIGHTHOOD

On Drake's return he was given a hero's welcome. He was knighted aboard his ship, the *Golden Hind*, by Elizabeth I the following year.

ILL FEELING

The serpent and beasts shown here are taken from a collection of engravings made to commemorate Drake's voyage. The serpent is a symbol of evil and bad luck, particularly to sailors. Drake kept his destination secret from his men, but when they eventually realized the truth they were urged to mutiny by Drake's one-time friend, Thomas Doughty, who was put on trial and executed.

DRAKE'S VOYAGE

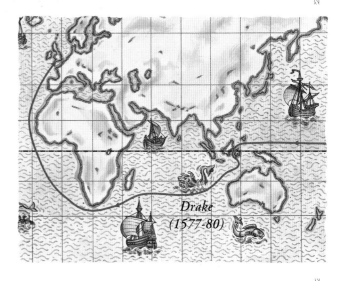

Drake (1577-80)

Although it is usually said that Magellan was the first person to sail round the world (1519-21) this is not true. He was the first European to cross the Pacific Ocean, but he never finished the circumnavigation. It is now thought that Magellan meant simply to sail to the East Indies via the Pacific. He returned home round the world to escape attack from the Portuguese, but was killed in the Philippines halfway through the journey. This means that Drake was actually the first commander to complete a circumnavigation, and so deserves more credit for this than he is sometimes given.

EXOTIC FOODS

Drake could not carry all the supplies he needed for his voyage, so rations were added on the way. The crew tried exotic foods from Central and South America and the Tropics. Drake brought these, and other foods back to England where they became popular among the rich. Some could be grown in England but pineapples, for example, needed to be grown in conservatories.

SECRET VOYAGE

Shortly before setting out, Drake was summoned to a secret meeting with Queen Elizabeth. She ordered him to raid the unprotected Spanish ports on the west coast of South America. Drake was very successful and Elizabeth made £300,000.

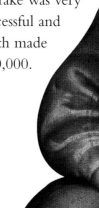

THE NEW COLONIES

The original idea for exploring new countries came from trade and the need to set-up new markets, and also from greed. Even the Spanish, who invaded parts of Central and South America, didn't think of colonization at first – what they wanted was gold. England, Holland and France were quick to follow, and plundered the Spanish ships returning home for their share of the booty. It was another 200 years before England made any serious attempts to build an empire. When it did, it followed the same pattern of setting up colonies around trading posts, with the result that the British Empire was spread across world trade routes.

VIRGINIA

England's first efforts at setting up colonies in North America laid the foundations of what one day was to become the British Empire. Walter Raleigh set up a small colony at Roanoke Island (now part of North Carolina) in 1584-5 and named the territory 'Virginia', in honour of Elizabeth – the 'virgin queen'. Conditions were harsh and the colony was deserted by 1590.

CONQUISTADORS

At the time of the first European colonization of Central and South America, there were two main civilizations there: the Aztecs, in what is now Mexico, and the Incas of Peru and surrounding areas. The Aztecs and the Incas attacked and conquered other societies. They charged high taxes, and often made human sacrifices, too. When the Spanish arrived in the 16th century, many welcomed them at first.

SAVED BY A PRINCESS

An early Virginian colonist, Captain John Smith, became friendly with an Indian princess, Pocahontas. Her father Powhattan, was said to be king of all the Indian tribes in the area. He wanted to kill the white colonists and return the land to the Indians. Pocahontas risked her life to warn Smith and avoided a massacre.

POCAHONTAS

Although Pocahontas saved the life of John Smith, he was injured and sent home to England. She later married another colonist, John Rolfe, and returned to England with him. Pocahontas persuaded Rolfe to let her return to America, but she died on the eve of her departure, aged 22. She is buried in Gravesend, Kent.

INDIANS' REVENGE

The Spanish gained control of Central and South America in just two years. There was plenty of gold and the conquerors plundered the lands searching for it. The Indians had welcomed the Spanish as their saviours at first, but the Spanish tortured and killed thousands of them. Many thousands more were forced to work in the mines. The Indians sometimes got their revenge, however. This picture shows them pouring molten gold down the throat of a captured *conquistador*.

THE SPANISH INVASION

One of the reasons for the success with which Spain overran the Aztec and Inca Empires is that many conquered Indian tribes actually helped the Spanish against their old enemies. Another reason was the Spanish use of guns, which were unknown in South America.

SEA TRADING

SLAVE TRADE

When the Spanish occupied the Caribbean and South America they treated the natives very badly, killing thousands. They also exported slaves from West Africa to work in the mines. The Spanish controlled this trade very strictly, but English sailors often traded slaves illegally.

Spain was then the richest and most powerful country in Europe and her empire already covered much of the West Indies and Central America. She controlled the southern and western seaway, so it was essential to open up new trade routes. Even though travelling by sea was dangerous, it was still better than overland transportation. Drake and the other Elizabethan sailors began by simply stealing Spanish treasure and other blatant acts of piracy, but soon the need to open up new and longer-term trade routes became the priority.

A SWEET TOOTH

Sugar cane was much better than the alternative – sugar beet – but would not grow in the English climate. Many sugar plantations were set up in the West Indies, usually using slave labour.

SOUTH CHINA SEAS

From the mid-16th century, trade between the Far East and Europe increased, and heavily-laden merchant ships were targets for pirates. The South China Seas between China, Japan and the East Indies were especially dangerous. Favourite vessels of Chinese pirates were trading junks, as shown here. Eventually, companies (such as the East India Company) persuaded the British government to protect merchant shipping.

RUSSIA

In 1553 Sir Hugh Willoughby and Richard Chancellor set out to try to discover the North-East Passage. They became separated: Willoughby died, but Chancellor went on to Moscow (shown here) the following year. He set up trade relations between Russia and England but died on a return trip in 1555.

UNUSUAL FOODS

Many of the foods brought back from trips were seen as interesting oddities, such as the tomato. Others, such as the potato, quickly became firm favourites. They were usually quite expensive, though, and were regarded as a treat.

SPICE IS NICE

Peppers and chillies, from South America (left), were used to disguise food that had gone off. During Drake's circumnavigation he had to take on board many unusual and exotic foods to feed his crew. Amongst these was the coconut palm, which natives used as a major source of food, making oil from the kernels.

TOBACCO FOR HEALTH?

Tobacco plants (above right) came from North America. Originally it was used as a medicine to rid the body of phlegm.

OCEAN ROUTES

SIR THOMAS GRESHAM
(C.1519-79)

The cost of voyages was very high and needed financial backing from rich merchants. One of these was Sir Thomas Gresham, who built the Royal Exchange in London.

*E*lizabethan expeditions reached countries as far apart as Russia, North America, Canada, South America, Africa and Asia looking for new trade routes. Their achievement was all the more incredible because of how long it took to complete the journeys in small ships, often crossing uncharted seas. Spices were highly prized and valuable, and sold for huge sums in markets around Europe.

The view shown here is of the tropical coast of Ceylon, (now Sri Lanka), off the south-east coast of India.

THE BEGINNINGS OF AN EMPIRE

India and Ceylon had been known to European explorers since at least c.1295 and would have been familiar to the Elizabethan sailors on their visits to the Spice Islands. As elsewhere, the Elizabethans' main concern was setting up new trade routes, but they often experienced strange new cultures, from Indian witch doctors in North America (shown here) to the highly sophisticated and ancient cultures of Asia. In 1601 the East India Company received its royal charter, marking the beginning of Britain's first claims to an empire.

LIFE ONBOARD

*L*ife onboard ship in Elizabethan time was very hard. The pay was poor and often late. However, those on the land were also suffering. Many people were very poor, and had little choice but to become sailors. The death rate at sea was high, and ships often returned to port with only a quarter of the men left alive. Captains signed up too many men to make sure there would be enough to sail home again, but this caused problems of overcrowding and food rationing. There was little room onboard and the men usually slept in hammocks slung below decks. There were no toilet facilities.

JACK-OF-ALL-TRADES

Crews had to be able to look after themselves. They were often away for several years, and might go many months between landings. As well as handling the ship, sailors also had to master other skills, such as carpentry, sailmaking, ropemaking and cooking.

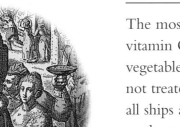

DRUNKENNESS

One of the main problems facing any captain on a long voyage was boredom. With fresh water in short supply, the only drink available was beer or other alcohol, which often led to drunkenness. Discipline had to be very harsh to avoid accidents at sea.

DISEASE

The most common disease was scurvy – a lack of vitamin C – from not eating enough fruit and vegetables. This often ended in death if not treated. Rats were a problem on all ships and spread diseases such as plague. Other diseases included malaria, typhoid and dysentery.

THE CHATHAM CHEST

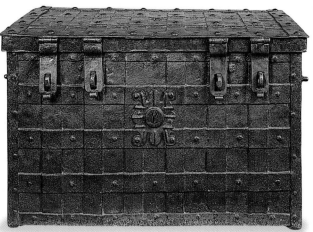

So many seamen were wounded in the battles with the Armada, that Sir John Hawkins set up the 'Chatham Chest' – the first seamen's charity.

THE GUNNER

Most Elizabethan ships carried a number of cannon (a mortar is shown here). They were fixed in place by heavy ropes to prevent them moving in heavy seas. They were used mostly to disable a ship before boarding.

HEALTH AND SAFETY

Accidents onboard were common and injuries during battles with enemy vessels were horrific. Most ships carried a surgeon, but the most common treatment was amputating badly damaged or infected limbs. There was no anaesthetic (apart from making the patient drunk) and the survival rate was very low.

DAILY SUSTENANCE

Ship's food was prepared in the galley and then handed out among the crew. Food was rarely fresh and might consist of biscuit, salted beef or fish, with cheese and gruel. Drinking water was usually limited but most ships carried a large supply of beer. The tableware shown here were found on Henry VIII's ship the *Mary Rose*, and are typical of items in use at this time.

EVENTS OF DRAKE'S LIFE

~1581~
Drake buys Buckland Abbey and is appointed Mayor of Plymouth

~1583~
John Somerville tries to assassinate Elizabeth

~1583~
Sir Humphrey Gilbert claims Newfoundland for England

~1584~
Walter Raleigh establishes the first colony in Virginia

~1585~
Drake's first command as Admiral

19

NAVIGATION

It is easy to forget about the great navigational skills of the Elizabethan sailors. Usually they were sailing uncharted seas and had to estimate their position as best they could, using only the positions of heavenly bodies to guide them. Until the development of better instruments, such as the chronometer in the mid-18th century, navigation was a very inexact science and relied heavily on the skills of the individual. There were many accidents, especially if the ships were blown off-course by bad weather into unknown waters.

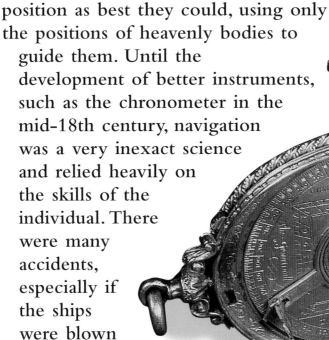

GUIDED BY THE STARS

In the 16th century a cross-staff was commonly used to calculate a ship's latitude (north-south position) at night. Above is a buckstaff, invented about 1594, for measuring the height of the sun for the same purpose.

THE MARINER'S MIRROUR

After Magellan's, and later Drake's, circumnavigation of the world, it became possible to estimate the Earth's size more accurately, and led to the production of more accurate charts. The first sea atlas to be published in England, in 1588, was the Mariner's Mirrour. It was a collection of maps and charts showing the known coastlines of the world, based on Dutch originals. The Dutch were at that time an English ally against Spain and were leaders in navigational techniques.

LODESTONE

One of the main problems facing Elizabethan navigators was accurately calculating a ship's longitude (east-west position). Here, the astronomer-mathematician Flavius tries to do so by floating a piece of lodestone (a magnetic mineral) in a bowl of water, whilst making calculations.

STEERING METHODS

This shows a navigator trying to calculate the ship's latitude using a compass, and an early form of quadrant to measure the angle of the sun's rays. At best, a ship's position could only be roughly judged without precise time-keeping.

DRAKE'S DIAL

Compasses and other astronomical instruments became quite complicated. This astronomical compendium made of brass in 1569 by Humphrey Cole may have belonged to Drake himself. It consisted of a compass, along with moon and sun dials. As well as being an astronomical aid, it could calculate the time.

EVENTS OF DRAKE'S LIFE

~1587~
The Spanish decide to launch offensive against England

Drake sacks the port of Cadiz - 'singing the King of Spain's beard'

~1588~
Spanish Armada defeated in the Channel after week-long battle

GETTING YOUR BEARINGS

The ancient Chinese discovered that lodestone is naturally magnetic, and if suspended on a string will always point to the north. Early navigators made good use of this natural material. Sometime in the 12th century, European navigators discovered that a needle could be similarly magnetised by stroking it with a lodestone. This discovery eventually led to the development of more accurate compasses. The example shown here dates from about 1580.

PITCHED BATTLE

The commander of the English fleet
sent to stop the Armada was Lord
Howard of Effingham. The battle
turned in favour of the English
when Drake launched eight fire-
ships into the Armada near
Calais. This threw the
Spanish into chaos. The
following day the Armada
was defeated
and fled into
the North Sea.

THE SPANISH ARMADA

After Henry VIII's break with the Church of Rome in 1533, England was under constant threat from the Catholic countries of Europe. Spain was angry at the acts of piracy on her ships by English adventurers, especially during Elizabeth I's reign, so was keen to attack England. In July 1588 a massive armada of 138 ships and 24,000 men was sent to invade England.

ARMADA MEDAL

This gold medal, commemorating England's victory over the Armada, was awarded to each of the commanders of the English fleet.

THE ARMADA APPROACHES

Drake is rumoured to have insisted on finishing his game of bowls before putting out to sea. The Spanish Armada created a frightening sight as it went slowly up the Channel. But the daring seamanship of Drake and many others won the day.

LATER LIFE

DRAKE'S LAST VOYAGE

Drake's last, doomed voyage took place in 1595-6. He and John Hawkins were sent to attack Puerto Rico, to cut off Spain's supply of treasure ships. Drake stopped at the Canary Islands (above) for supplies. A messenger ship was sent from the Canaries to warn the governor of Puerto Rico of the attack. With two weeks' warning, the Spanish were prepared and the attack failed. Hawkins died before the attack was launched, and Drake about a month later, of dysentery off Porto Bello on 25 January 1596.

Although Drake has often been accused of being little better that a legalized pirate, such criticism is perhaps a little harsh. He was an honourable man, who took good care of his crews. After his circumnavigation, he became Mayor of Plymouth and campaigned for many improvements to the town, including a better water supply. A short man of stocky build, he is said to have become quite fat in later life, and settled into semi-retirement at Buckland Abbey, near his birthplace. This had been seized by the crown at the dissolution and converted into a fine house by Sir Richard Grenville.

DRAKE'S DRUM

"Take my drum to England, hang et by the shore,
Strike et when your powder's runnin' low;
If the Dons sight Devon, I'll quit the port o' Heaven,
An' drum them up the Channel as we drummed
them long ago"

These lines are taken from a poem by Sir Henry Newbolt. The drum was used aboard the *Golden Hind* to muster the crew for battle. On his deathbed, Drake according to legend, promised to return and fight for England if ever the drum were beaten at the approach of an enemy.

BRILLIANT STRATEGIST

Throughout his brilliant career Drake was greatly feared by the Spanish. In 1587 he carried out a perfect attack on Cadiz Harbour, where he was said to have 'singed the King of Spain's beard' – destroying 37 galleons to be sent against England. The following year, of course, he was important in defeating the Armada itself, and was also a constant threat to Spanish shipping in the Caribbean. An expert navigator, he revolutionized naval strategy by taking the fight to the enemy. When Philip II of Spain heard of his death, he is said to have rejoiced.

FALL FROM FAVOUR

In 1583 Drake's first wife died. Soon after, he married Elizabeth Sydenham but had no children by either wife. He slipped into semi-retirement after the defeat of the Armada in 1588 and spent more and more time either at court, or in his new official duties at Plymouth. Martin Frobisher soon took over from him as Elizabeth's shining star.

OTHER EXPLORERS

The 'age of discovery' by European explorers really began in Portugal, in 1415, with Prince Henry, known as Henry the Navigator. He sent ships out to explore the north and west coasts of Africa, bringing back such riches as ivory. Vasco da Gama (c.1460-1524), also Portuguese, rounded the Cape of Good Hope, off the southernmost tip of Africa, and went on to open the first European route to India. Later Portuguese explorers went on to discover routes to Japan, south-east Asia and South America, which soon made Portugal one of the wealthiest nations in Europe. Apart from progress made in making more accurate navigational charts, very little scientific facts were gathered on these early voyages.

ARAB INFLUENCE

Between the 6th and 13th centuries Arab explorers from north Africa extended their empire. They developed astronomical equipment, such as this astrolabe, which greatly influenced European explorers.

JOHN CABOT (c.1450-99)

The search for new trade routes for England really began with Henry VII. He financed an expedition by the Italian John Cabot, to find a new route to China and the Spice Islands via the fabled North-West Passage. He believed he had reached China when he struck land, but it was in fact the coast of Newfoundland. He is seen here leaving Bristol in 1497.

CHURCH MISSIONARIES

Within a few years of the first expeditions, Christian missionaries were established to convert the 'pagan natives'. Many became victims of these natives, like the Franciscan missionaries here being eaten by North American cannibals.

THE SHIPWRIGHT'S SKILL

Sir John Hawkins introduced new ship designs by Matthew Baker and Peter Pett, which improved the English navy greatly. The new ships were smaller, faster and easier to handle than the huge Spanish galleons.

CELESTIAL GLOBE

This Flemish celestial globe (c.1537) shows the limited understanding of the southern hemisphere. Information gathered from the voyages of Magellan, Drake and others was added later, but this lack of knowledge made any journey in the southern oceans especially dangerous.

EVENTS OF DRAKE'S LIFE

~1591~

Sir Richard Grenville dies after being surrounded by Spanish in Azores

~1594~

Martin Frobisher dies

~1595~

Drake sets off to attack Puerto Rico (his last voyage) with John Hawkins

NO SMOKE WITHOUT FIRE

Raleigh may not have introduced potatoes and tobacco to England, he did however make smoking fashionable at court. It was usually smoked in long clay pipes. Raleigh is seen here being soaked with water by one of his servants, who feared he was on fire!

SIR WALTER RALEIGH (C.1552-1618)

Sir Walter Raleigh was a soldier, courtier and explorer. He was keen to set up English colonies in the New World, including Virginia, but they all failed. When James I came to the throne he was accused of treason and imprisoned.

SIR JOHN HAWKINS (1532-95)

Sir John Hawkins played a major role in defeating the Spanish Armada. Together with Drake, he set up a fund for distressed seamen called the Chatham Chest. He is said to have introduced the potato and tobacco into England. He died in 1595 during his and Drake's last Caribbean voyage.

EVENTS OF DRAKE'S LIFE

~1595~

Sir John Hawkins dies

~1596~

Drake dies of dysentery at Porto Bello in the Caribbean

THE SEARCH FOR *EL DORADO*

In 1616 Raleigh persuaded James I to let him lead an expedition to Guiana, to search for *El Dorado* (city of gold). The voyage failed and Raleigh came home in disgrace. He was executed in 1618.

OCEAN PIONEERS

The world in the 15th century was very different from today. There were areas of advanced civilization, including North Africa, the Mediterranean, China and India, but they had very little knowledge of each other. Few Europeans knew about the world beyond Europe. The Atlantic Ocean was largely unexplored, and it had not been proved that America and the Pacific Ocean really existed. For the brave few setting out on voyages of discovery, it was a journey into the unknown, rather like modern-day space explorations to the moon and beyond.

SIR RICHARD GRENVILLE (C.1541-91)

Grenville was another who wanted to colonize the New World rather than simply attacking Spanish treasure ships. He is best remembered for his brave fight off Flores, in the Azores, in 1591. He commanded the *Revenge* – Drake's former flagship – against the Armada. A proud man, he was wounded and ordered the ship to be sunk rather than give it up to the Spanish, but his crew surrendered. Grenville died aboard the Spanish flagship shortly afterwards.

SIR HUMPHREY GILBERT (C.1539-83)

Gilbert was also a supporter of English colonies in the New World. In 1583, he set off for Newfoundland. At St John's – already a lively port – he claimed the territory for England. He died on the way home, leaving his half-brother, Walter Raleigh, to finish his task.

DANGEROUS JOURNEYS

*F*or us today, it is difficult to understand how huge the Elizabethan voyages of exploration were. The men who made them were very brave. Most of the European countries were at war and therefore acted independently of each other. At this time, England was not an important country – scientific discoveries and the empire came much later. On these voyages, not only did the adventurers plunder foreign lands, they also spread disease. Four hundred years on, we can see the huge impact these early explorers made on our knowledge of the world.

SIR MARTIN FROBISHER (C.1535-94)

In 1576 Martin Frobisher set out to discover the North–West Passage and a trading route to China. He failed in this and two other attempts, but he did make many important discoveries in the Arctic Ocean, including Baffin Island. Along with Drake and Hawkins, he was a key figure in the defeat of the Spanish Armada in 1588. He died of gangrene from a bullet wound got chasing the Spanish out of the port of Brest, northern France.

STRANGE SIGHTS

Explorers in the 16th century saw many strange cultures, plants and animals never before seen by Europeans. The women shown here (probably from Java) are killing themselves after the death of their king, an act seen by Cavendish in 1586-88.

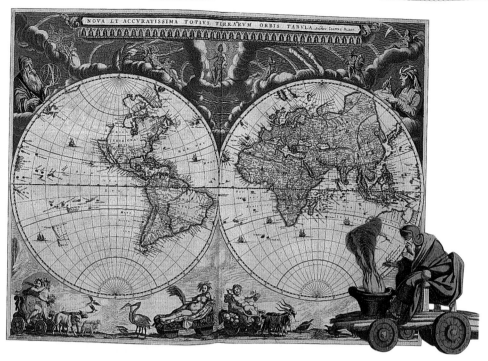

MAP OF THE PIRATE SEAS

The first expeditions by English mariners were little more than acts of legalized piracy. Elizabeth I instructed her sea captains to stop as many Spanish treasure ships as possible and steal their gold. Afterwards, when the expeditions became ones of discovery, the seas remained full of pirates who attacked any ship and plundered its cargo.

ARMAMENTS

Most ships in the 16th century carried guns similar to this bronze demi-cannon found in the wreck of the *Mary Rose*, which sank in 1545. Cannon of this type remained the main form of armament on fighting ships for the next 300 years.

THOMAS CAVENDISH (1560-92)

Shortly after Drake's return, Thomas Cavendish was asked to repeat his voyage. He followed the same route, but in less time. His was probably the first planned circumnavigation. In 1591 Cavendish set out again for the East Indies, but the voyage ended in disaster and around three quarters of the crew died from scurvy.

GLOSSARY

Armada A fleet of warships. The Spanish Armada was a naval invasion planned by King Philip II of Spain against England.

Armillary sphere A model of the world with hoops to mark the Equator and Tropics which revolves on its axis.

Astronomical Something related to the science of celestial objects (stars, comets, planets) space and the universe.

Circumnavigation Sailing all the way around the world.

Dysentery A serious infection of the intestines which can lead to death if not treated. It can be caused by infected food or water.

Equator An imaginary line drawn around the Earth which divides it in half.

Gangrene A serious infection caused by bacteria. It could lead to death if not treated.

Hemisphere Half of a globe. The Earth is divided into a northern hemisphere and a southern hemisphere by the Equator.

Junk A flat-bottomed sailing ship popular in China and the East Indies.

Mutiny To rebel or refuse to obey orders. It is most commonly used to refer to sailors refusing to obey their captains.

Privateer Sea captains who have permission from the ruling monarch to attack the ships of another country and steal their cargoes.

Scurvy A disease caused by a lack of vitamin C, from not eating enough fresh fruit and vegetables. It could lead to death if not treated.

Singed To lightly burn something.

ACKNOWLEDGEMENTS

Consultant Editor: Pieter van der Merwe, National Maritime Museum. We would also like to thank: Graham Rich, Peter Done, Rosie Hankin and Elizabeth Wiggans for their assistance and David Hobbs for his map of the world.

Copyright © 2008 ticktock Entertainment Ltd.

First published in Great Britain by ticktock Publishing Ltd., Unit 2, Orchard Business Centre, North Farm Road, Tunbridge Wells, Kent TN2 3XF in association with the National Maritime Museum, Greenwich.

All rights reserved. No part of this publication may be reproduced, stored in a retrieval system, or transmitted in any form or by any means, electronic, mechanical, photocopying, recording or otherwise, without prior written permission of the copyright owner.

A CIP catalogue record for this book is available from the British Library.

ISBN 978 1 84696 657 6

Picture research by Image Select.

Printed in China.

Picture Credits: t=top, b=bottom, c=centre, l=left, r=right, OFC=outside front cover, OBC=outside back cover, IFC=inside front cover

Aisa (Barcelona): IFC 1 tl, 12 tl. Ann Ronan / Image Select (London): 18/19 cb. Bridgeman (London): 3 tl, 3 bl, 25 cr, 28 cb. The Golden Hinde Ltd (London): 10/11 c & OFC. Image Select: 8 bl, 15 tr. Mary Evans Picture Library: 1 tr, 3 cr, 4 t, 5 br, 6 c, 6 tr, 6/7 c, 6/7 cb, 7 br, 8/9 cb, 9 cb, 10 t, 10 bl, 12 bl & 13 br, 13 t, 12/13 cb, 14 tl & OFC, 14 bl, 15 r & OFC, 16/17, 16 t & OBC, 17 tl & OFC, 18 tl, 18 bl, 19 c, 21 tr, 20/21 ct, 22 tr & OBC, 24 tl, 24/25 c, 25 tr, 26 bl, 28 tr & OBC, 28/29 cb, 30/31 cb, 31 br, 32 c. National Maritime Museum (London): IFC, 25 l & tr & 32 c, 2 br, 3 bl, 5 cl, 8 cl, 10 br, 11 br & OFC, 12/13 c & OFC, 14/15 c & OBC, 18/19 ct & OBC, 19 tr, 20 tl, 20/21 c & OBC, 21 br & OBC, 20 tl, 20 bl, 22/23, 23 tr, 22 cr, 24 bl & OBC, 26 tl, 26/27 cb, OFC & IFC, 27 t, 28 tl, 28 c & OBC, 29 br, 30 l, 30/31 c, 31t. PIX: 4 br, 9 c. Spectrum Colour Library: 13 tr. Courtesy of The Ulster Museum (Belfast): 8/9 ct. West Devon Borough Council: 2 bl.

Every effort has been made to trace the copyright holders and we apologize in advance for any unintentional omissions. We would be pleased to insert the appropriate acknowledgement in any subsequent edition of this publication.